A Note to Parent

DK READERS is a compelling program for beginning readers, designed in conjunction with leading literacy experts, including Dr. Linda Gambrell, Distinguished Professor of Education at Clemson University. Dr. Gambrell has served as President of the National Reading Conference, the College Reading Association, and the International Reading Association.

Beautiful illustrations and superb full-color photographs combine with engaging, easy-to-read stories to offer a fresh approach to each subject in the series. Each DK READER is guaranteed to capture a child's interest while developing his or her reading skills, general knowledge, and love of reading.

The five levels of DK READERS are aimed at different reading abilities, enabling you to choose the books that are exactly right for your child:

Pre-level 1: Learning to read
Level 1: Beginning to read
Level 2: Beginning to read alone
Level 3: Reading alone
Level 4: Proficient readers

The "normal" age at which a child begins to read can be anywhere from three to eight years old. Adult participation through the lower levels is very helpful for providing encouragement, discussing storylines, and sounding out unfamiliar words.

No matter which level you select, you can be sure that you are helping your child learn to read, then read to learn!

LONDON, NEW YORK, MUNICH,
MELBOURNE, AND DELHI

Project Editors Caroline Bingham
and Penny Smith
Designer Michelle Baxter
US Editor Regina Kahney
Production Siu Chan
Jacket Designer Natalie Godwin
Editorial Consultant
Theresa Greenaway
Editor, this edition Anneka Wahlhaus
Art Director Rachael Foster
Publishing Manager Bridget Giles

Reading Consultant
Linda B. Gambrell, Ph.D.

First American edition, 1998
This edition, 2009
10 11 12 13 10 9 8 7 6 5 4 3 2
Published in the United States by DK Publishing
375 Hudson Street, New York, New York 10014

Published in Great Britain by Dorling Kindersley Limited.

DK books are available at special discounts when purchased
in bulk for sales promotions, premiums,
fund-raising, or educational use.
For details, contact: DK Publishing Special Markets
375 Hudson Street, New York, New York 10014
SpecialSales@dk.com

A catalog record for this book is available
from the Library of Congress

ISBN: 978-0-7566-5604-1 (pb)
ISBN: 978-0-7566-5606-5 (plc)

Color reproduction by Colourscan, Singapore
Printed and bound in China by L. Rex Printing Co. Ltd.

Photography by Paul Bricknell, Jane Burton, Geoff Dann, Mike
Dunning, Neil Fletcher, Frank Greenaway, Kim Taylor

All other images © Dorling Kindersley Limited
For further information see: www.dkimages.com

Discover more at
www.dk.com

DK READERS

BEGINNING TO READ

1

Tale of a Tadpole

Written by Karen Wallace

DK Publishing

The tale of a tadpole
begins in a pond.
Mother frog lays her eggs
next to a lily pad.

jelly

Each tiny egg
is wrapped
in clear jelly.

Inside the jelly
the eggs grow into tadpoles.
They wriggle like worms.

They push through the jelly
and swim in the water.

They breathe through gills,
just like fishes.

gills

Many other animals
live in the pond.

Shiny goldfish
and sticklebacks.
And great diving beetles.

They chase the young tadpoles.

A stickleback feels hungry.
He opens his mouth wide.

The little gray tadpoles
wriggle their tails ...

... and swim away
through the water.

A great diving beetle
feels hungry too.

His hairy back legs
beat through the water.

The tadpoles escape
and hide in the weeds.

Soon a tadpole
grows legs
with tiny webbed toes.

webbed
toes

Webbed toes are like flippers.
They help the small tadpole
push through the water.

He grows arms
with long skinny fingers.

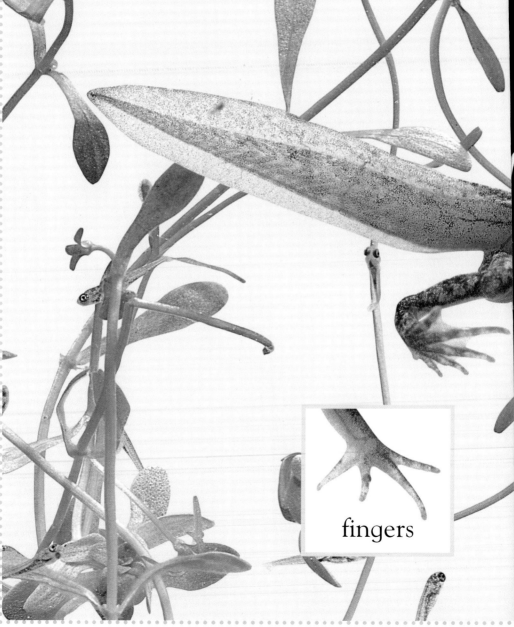

fingers

He nibbles on plants and gobbles green pondweed.

Half tadpole, half frog,
he rests in the sunshine.

His tail is shrinking.

tail

It gets smaller and smaller.

The new little frog
sits on a lily pad.

His legs are strong now.
He can breathe through his nostrils.
His skin is dotted
with tiny gold spots.

nostril

Frogs must keep their skin slimy.
He hops back in the pond
and swims for a while.
Then he climbs onto a log.

Another frog climbs up
and sits down beside him.

Now full-grown,
he dives through the water.

He's not afraid of the stickleback.
He swims past the beetle.

In the pond
he watches and waits.
What does he see
with his round beady eye?

eye

A fly lands
above him.
He creeps
closer and closer.

But a big frog jumps up.
It snatches the fly
with its long, sticky tongue.

tongue

The frog
misses his meal.
Next time
he'll be faster!

The golden-skinned frog
chases a dragonfly.
It lands on a lily pad.
Under the lily pad are
hundreds of frogs' eggs.

Inside each egg
a tadpole is growing.
Each tadpole will grow
into a golden-skinned frog.

Picture Word List

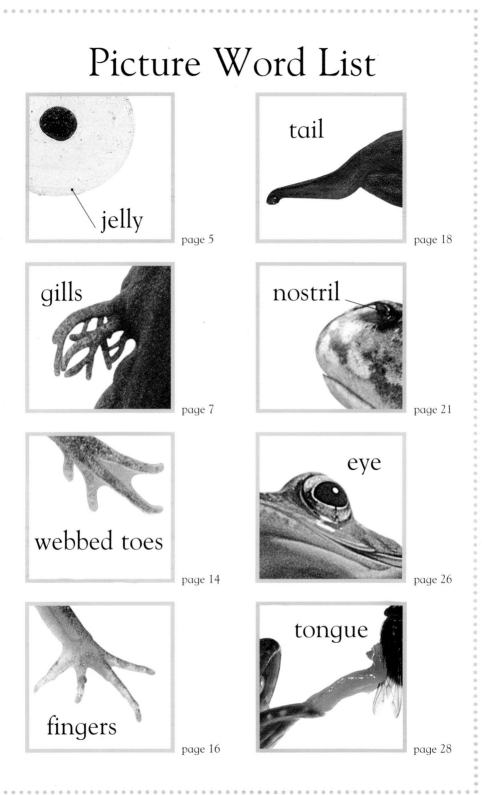

jelly

page 5

tail

page 18

gills

page 7

nostril

page 21

webbed toes

page 14

eye

page 26

fingers

page 16

tongue

page 28